Elephants do not float on Clouds?
Welcome to the Information Age

Jeffrey Lush –
Jeffrey.l.lush@gmail.com

First Printing: January 2019

ISBN: 978-0-359-36664-4

Purchase printed book, or other titles at: http://www.lulu.com, Barnes and Noble or Amazon.com. Search for Jeffrey Lush.

Contents

Welcome to the Information Age

Information technology presents unique challenges, which simply do not exist in other parts of our lives. Can you imagine placing different tire manufactures and tire sizes on your vehicle? How about a different door handle and lock for each room in your home? Of course not: the performance of your vehicle would suffer due to the varied tire sizes; and key management in your home would become a daunting task. As crazy as different tires and locks may sound, many consumers are building data analytic environments on existing technology or investing a fortune in "new technology" only to discover that it will not support their data analytic needs. For the next several pages we will review specific challenges and opportunities related to building surviving in the Information Age.

It is always easier to discuss new technology as it would apply to a consumer of the technology. The content of the paper will use GVL as an example. GVL has a unique stewardship to care for Earth, and the execution of their responsibilities illustrates the great advantages that can come from data analytics. The information related to GVL is extracted from the GVL Strategic Plans, published objectives and budget requests, the paper is simply using GVL as an example and can be applicable to many organizations. Examples and references will be reviewed throughout the book with the hope that you can relate the information to your environment.

System Management

System Management impacts all areas of our information technology environment. We will explore the integration of legacy and emerging technologies, consistency within the environment, and strategies to maintain a repeatable infrastructure. System management also includes operating tasks such as patch management, inventory and ITIL related practices.

- *Core Foundation*: just as the stability of a building is dependent upon a solid foundation, information technology architecture is dependent upon components found within the infrastructure, to include: servers, storage, network, firewalls, and many other components. A solid foundation enables us to provide these core technologies, and a way forward that increases performance and stabilizes cost.

- *Delivering Technology*: the delivery of technology is dependent upon our ability to effectively manage and provide a foundation required by our services. The delivery includes technologies like cloud, mobility and hosted desktop infrastructure. Enablement of the technology is dependent upon the organizations willingness to embrace software defined infrastructure, automated provisioning/orchestration, and a dynamic, resilient and tenacious security strategy.
- *Security*: security will continue to be a driving force for the Information Age. Security threats are no longer isolated to malware or viruses but are a constant threat. Successful organizations implement risk management frameworks (RMF), SIEM technologies for log aggregation, and proactive/preventive security analytics.

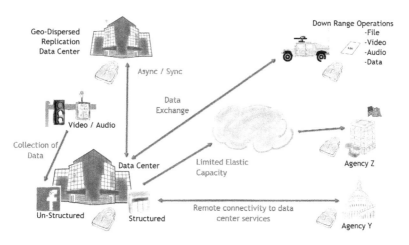

The objective of this book is to expose the reader to new concepts that build efficiency and stabilize cost for an enterprise architecture. Many enterprise infrastructures have been established for decades. Although, the demands of the enterprise architecture have changed dramatically over the past several years. Security is a dynamic, aggressive opponent. Data analytics will continue to be part of our lives, and mobility will continue to change the traditional approach to information technology. Found within the Sample Enterprise Architecture is a suggested enterprise architecture. Welcome to the Information Age.

Chapter 1: System Management

Let's start by establishing a baseline of functional requirements. Functional requirements declare tangible results and objectives. Functional requirements motivate us to look a little deeper, to solve business challenges without the distraction of attractive features and/or limitations of a manufacturer's strength and/or weakness. For the benefit of this exercise we will use a fictitious organization called: GVL. To make the discussion relevant: we have a mix of x86 servers from Dell, IBM and HP. Network, Firewall and Storage include CISCO, Brocade, EMC and 3PAR.

With limited details about the specific configuration of the environment, the following assumptions have been made. Information Technology specialists can collect and provide this information about your environment. Systems management is at the core of any enterprise architecture designed for optimal performance and price stabilization; without systems management: enterprise architecture is often inefficient and costly.

Step 1: Gather the Customer Requirements

GVL is looking for a more efficient way to manage their infrastructure. Some of the details of the GVL environment include:

- Server infrastructure, primarily from a single vendor (HP), dating back 5 generations of servers (non-blade servers).

- Management of the environment should be orchestrated through GVLs implementation of Microsoft System Center Operations Manager (SCOM).

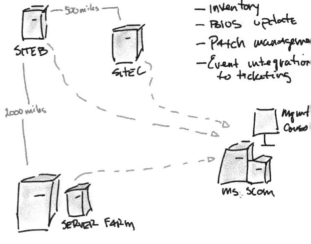

- Multiple HP servers within multiple data centers, all geographically dispersed throughout the globe.
- Due to security restrictions, much of the infrastructure is unable to communicate on the public internet, hence an offline solution must be available.

Step 2: Review the Functional Requirements

With this information, GVL has stated the following functional requirements:

- Collect an accurate inventory for all infrastructure components. Inventory should include the standard WMI (Windows Management Information).
- Automate and deploy BIOS updates to servers and log results.
- Patch Management of the operating system and applications.
- Events should automatically integrate with the (NSOC) help desk.

System Management will reduce cost

Several technologies come into consideration when discussing IT enterprise management. As new standards emerge, the industry in general rallies to support the standard. As software developers / OEMs (ie: HP, Dell, Cisco, IBM) embrace the standard, it becomes "publicly available" as an "Open Standard". Some vendors will provide enhanced functionality creating a "locked down" version/standard for their equipment only. While vendor specific technology may be advantageous to a specific vendor, an "Open Standard" approach typically renders a more integrated management infrastructure, amid the reality that most environments are not isolated to a single vendor. Understanding the core technology for system management may assist in understanding the solutions provided by vendors. Listed are a few key core technologies, organizations and lexicon:

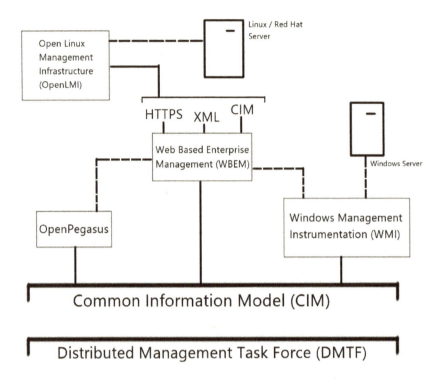

Open Linux Management Infrastructure (OpenLMI)

Linux / Red Hat Server

HTTPS XML CIM

Web Based Enterprise Management (WBEM)

Windows Server

OpenPegasus

Windows Management Instrumentation (WMI)

Common Information Model (CIM)

Distributed Management Task Force (DMTF)

DMTF (Distributed Management Task Force)

DMTF is an organization bringing the IT industry together to collaborate on systems management standards development, validation, promotion and adoption. A recent example is OVF. OVF takes advantage of the DMTF's (CIM), where appropriate, to allow management software to clearly understand and easily map resource properties by using an open standard.

CIM (Common Information Model)

CIM Specification defines the details for integration with other management models. CIM is built on the concept of management schemas, the building blocks for management platforms and applications. The CIM model has been around since 2005, providing a common standard for system management.

WBEM (Web Based Enterprise Management)

Web-Based Enterprise Management (WBEM) is a set of specifications published by DMTF that define how resources modeled using the DMTF's Common Information Model (CIM) can be discovered, accessed and manipulated. WBEM provides the ability for the industry to deliver a well-integrated set of standard-based management tools, facilitating the exchange of data across otherwise disparate technologies and platforms.

WMI (Windows Management Instrumentation)

WMI works great for environments that are running Windows Operating Systems, although does not work with other operating systems. WMI is the CIM offering to support Windows Operating Systems. WMI is Microsoft's support of WBEM (see below) in alignment with the Distributed Management Task Force (see below).

OpenLMI (Open Linux Management Infrastructure)

OpenLMI is the CIM offering to support Red Hat Operating Systems. Similar in function to WMI.

SNMP (Simple Network Management Protocol)

A very common protocol used that supports Windows, Red Hat and other operating systems. A query against the SNMP collection will expose a lot of information by default. Some environments do not allow SNMP to be active, hence alternatives like WMI and OpenLMI are available.

REST (Representational State Transfer)

REST is a simple and stateless architecture that generally runs over HTTP. For many, it is the "preferred protocol" to SOAP (Simple Object Access Protocol) as REST leverages very little bandwidth which makes it a better protocol to transfer over the internet. REST's decoupled architecture and lighter weight communication between producer and consumer, make REST very popular for cloud-based APIs. REST is becoming the "dial tone" for system interaction.

Now that we understand the key attributes of systems management, as well as the standards that have been in place for over a decade, we can begin to formulate our functionality and visualization strategy to accommodate a wide range of servers within our environment.

Functional Enterprise Management

When I purchase a new vehicle, it is not uncommon for me to replace the wheels and tires. Often, I replace the tires based on the terrain and/or conditions that may require a different performance level than the tire was designed for. Tire replacement is dictated by my "functional requirement". Sometimes the new tires require a different wheel to meet my functional requirement, although more than not, the wheel is replaced because of my personal preference and/or comfort with a specific type of wheel. When managing an infrastructure, we must declare the functional requirements first, and then evaluate tools in the environment to discover potential gaps that need to be filled. Just as in the tire and wheel example, the functional replacement of the tire may be required, although the wheel may work out just fine. In the absence of functional requirements, it will be difficult to provide technology to meet the long-term objectives for the organization.

Step 3: Exploring "System Management" options

One of the challenges in managing GVL's environment is the wide range of infrastructure, and varied age of the equipment, that current makes up the GVL environment. It is not uncommon for management solutions to have limits as to the generation/age of the infrastructure that is supported. GVL has infrastructure that dates back almost a decade so to meet the stated customer objectives we will need to get a little creative. Equally as challenging is often a requirement for specific configuration levels (ie: BIOS) to be achieved prior to full management functionality. Sometimes this can be difficult in large environments that have not updated infrastructure as frequently as they should. Listed are a few HP server management tools as an example that will help GVL meet the functional and business requirements for systems management. The HP tools are suggested as HP is a predominant server technology for many environments. Dell, IBM and others have similar toolsets. Use the HP tools for GVL example as a starting point for your research of other tools in the market.

- HP Systems Insight Manager (HP SIM) is the easiest, simplest, least expensive solution to manage HP servers. It provides inventory, health management and firmware and driver updates, and integrates with HP OneView, HP Insight Control and Matrix Operating Environment.

(http://goo.gl/3CpuhU) . For a complete list of supported servers and devices in SIM: http://goo.gl/4zcpaq

- HP Insight Control is essential management for HP infrastructure. Insight Control integrates capabilities into HP Systems Insight Manager to manage server health and alerting, deploy and migrate servers quickly, optimize power consumption and performance, and control servers from anywhere. Integration with VMware vCenter Server and Microsoft System Center is also enabled for single-console management of physical and virtual environments.

- HP OneView for Microsoft System Center (previously known as HP Insight Control for Microsoft System Center) provides seamless integration of the unique HP ProLiant and HP BladeSystem manageability features into Microsoft System Center. Licensed with HP OneView and HP Insight Control, these extensions deliver comprehensive system health and alerting, driver and firmware updates, OS deployment, detailed inventory, and HP fabric visualization.

- HP Insight Diagnostics is a tool with limited application to the stated customer objectives, although may be able to contact the older server generations. HP Insight Diagnostics Online Edition is a web-based application that captures hardware and operating system configuration information, records critical information for documentation and disaster recovery, and compares historical configurations on the same server or a baseline server.

Step 4: Take a closer look at Systems Management

Now that we understand the HP tools (HP System Insight Manager (SIM), HP Insight Control, HP OneView and HP Insight Diagnostics) that are available to GVL for systems management, let's take a closer look at the functionality of the tools. Dependent upon your environment and vendor choice, use the illustrated functional requirements as a starting point for the placement of the correct tool in your environment. It is important to note that the functionality listed is not "all inclusive", although should represent many of the functional requirements for GVL.

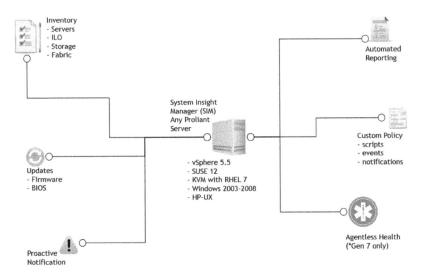

Details: HP System Insight Manager (SIM)

SIM is a tool that will support all the HP servers in the GVL environment. It has some very basic functionality that meets the stated objectives for GVL. It is important to note that the drawing does not include all features. If a specific server generation is not listed: often older generations may work, although updates have been discontinued to focus on more recent hardware platform generations.

Details: HP OneView

HP OneView supports older generation of servers, as well as many components within the infrastructure. It is important to note all the features and how they can benefit GVL.

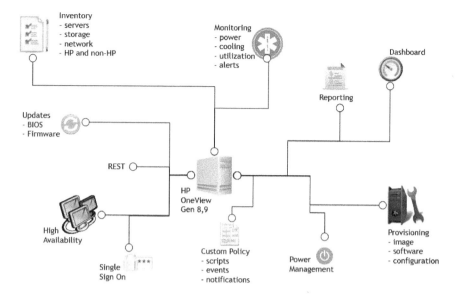

Step 5: Pros and Cons of Systems Management

It is difficult to have a single tool be everything to everyone. All tools, whether they are "add-on tools" or "integrated tools" all have their strength and areas of improvement.

What is the difference between an "add-on tool" and an "integrated tool"?

- **Integrated Tool:** When a computer boots, the BIOS prompts the "loader" to start a sequence of events, often resulting in the instantiation of the operating system for use by the consumer. The loader in this example is an integrated tool. In the past several years the market has seen the introduction of converged infrastructure. Converged infrastructure often leverages an integrated tool model, wherein a function is being performed, although you may not be aware of the actual "tool" performing the function.

- *Add-on tool:* The tools we have discussed herein are add-on tools. An add-on tool is a tool that you are aware of, that is performing a function within your environment. Microsoft SCOM is another example of an add-on tool.

Add-on vs Integrated Tool

A variable to consider is the add-on vs integrated tool. Some food for thought: An integrated tool in some instances may be advantageous, although very focused on specific tasks, whereas an add-on tool typically provides a wider range of functionality and customization.

As stated, rarely will a single management tool provide everything that you are seeking within your environment. More often we must decide as to the functionality, cost and effort associated with the management tool.

Step 6: Evaluate your System Management needs

The weighted evaluation looks at three areas: **effort** to implement the function (indirect to cost), **function** of the specific objective (does it work in the environment) and **relevance** is the functional objective

Objective	Effort (0-10)	Function (0-10)	Relevant (0-10)
Collect WMI	10	10	10
Collect OpenLMI	0	0	2
BIOS Updates	10	10	10
Event/Alerts	7	10	10
SCOM integtation	9	10	10
Custom Scripts	10	10	7
Power Monitoring	10	10	10
Remote Control	10	10	5
Firmware Update	10	10	10
P-V Migration	6	10	5
Workload Migration	6	10	5
Bare Metal Provisioing	6	10	5
Automated Reporting	3	3	5
XML export	0	0	0
Agentless Health	0	0	0
Proactive Notification	7	5	10
Power Management	10	10	5
Single Signon	0	0	5
Multiple HP Servers	10	10	10
Software Provisioning	0	0	0
Dashboard	0	0	0

relevant to our environment. You can download the evaluation spreadsheet at: https://goo.gl/TEt4tZ (you will need to select the DOWNLOAD arrow to view as an excel spreadsheet). An example from another customer, GVL will need to complete the spreadsheet to match the requirements of their environment.

Weighted Evaluation

The weighted evaluation is to align objectives to tool functionality. To gather the real opinion of an organization, distribute the evaluation independently to each team member in a non-collaborative approach. Collect the information from the evaluation, then compare. If needed, bring the team together to discuss the results. This approach allows an organization to be more functional focused rather than product focused. A firm foundation will help all organizations to build a secure, predictable and manageable environment.

The numeric value is dictated by the individual completing the evaluation, it does not always represent functionality of the actual software tool, but rather the individuals understanding of the

Weighted Values	Actual	Possible
Effort	124	200
Function	138	200
Relevance	124	200

	Actual	Possible
Overall Score	386	600
Desirable Percentage		64%

* the higher the score/percentage, the most desirable.

functional' of the software tool. Leveraging the evaluation tool above, or another process within your organization, conduct an interview. The evaluation will provide a level playing field for all related technologies and decision variables that are critical to a cost-effective conclusion.

Step 7: Taking Action

The GVL environment is a geo-dispersed environment with infrastructure that dates back almost a decade. We have discussed the concept behind systems management, the tools for GVL, as well as some decision criteria for evaluating a system management architecture.

Chapter 2: Building a Core Foundation

The following pages we will review a few of the technologies and strategies that form a predictable, performance oriented, cost stabilized enterprise infrastructure.

- **Network**: network infrastructure should provide performance and security, as well as drive down operational cost. We will explore network technology strategies to include: software defined networking (SDN), open standard protocols like OpenFlow, and high availability both local and geo-dispersed.

- **Storage**: storage today, and in the future will continue to consume operational cost. Many environments report that storage represents one third of their operating budget. We will spend some time discussing ways to stabilize storage costs, while maintaining performance, manageability, and scalability.

- **Compute**: when you think about servers in the GVL environment, it is not uncommon to consider 1U, 2U and 4U servers, or perhaps blade server enclosures. Consider the collapse of the compute footprint, all the way down to the mobile device. The past several years has introduced new technologies to reduce server footprint, simplify server management and deployment, reduce energy costs, and provide focused computer platforms for specific workloads, while maintaining open standards.

There are many components found within an enterprise architecture. The three mentioned above: network, storage, compute often represent the lion share of cost and stability within our environments.

Looking at the Network

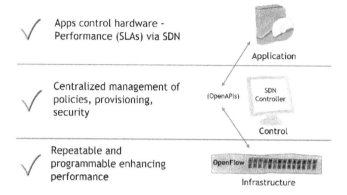

Apps control hardware - Performance (SLAs) via SDN ✓

Centralized management of policies, provisioning, security ✓

Repeatable and programmable enhancing performance ✓

For many enterprise environments, the network represents a substantial cost. In addition to cost, the network is the frontline for security tactics. To remain agile amid an ever-growing security threat, the network must be flexible, responsive, and ready to adjust at a moment's notice.

Software defined networking, or often referred to as SDN, continues to leverage your existing network infrastructure, although introduces control of the infrastructure via software, called the SDN controller.

In addition to simplifying your network infrastructure, SDN presents the opportunity for an organization to "commoditize" their network gear. The word commoditize in this context refers to the ability an organization has to reduce/eliminate their dependency upon

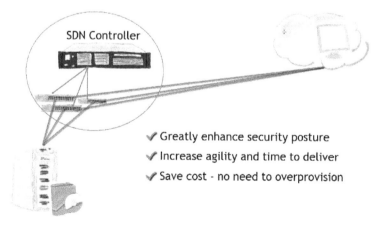

SDN Controller

✓ Greatly enhance security posture
✓ Increase agility and time to deliver
✓ Save cost - no need to overprovision

any specific network manufacturer. Leveraging network equipment enabled with OpenFlow, allows an organization to purchase network gear based on functionality and not vendor "lock-in".

I appreciate that for many environments the network infrastructure is taboo, never to be altered. Although I submit for consideration, the implementation of SDN will drive down operational cost considerably. Reduce your dependency upon a single vendor, and enter into a competitive network manufacturer world, absent of "expensive vendor specific skill sets", and annual maintenance contracts.

Enhance your security profile SDN by providing the technology and policies to adjust to emerging threats and vulnerabilities. To learn more about SDN, go to: https://goo.gl/ITIaWc for brief YouTube videos.

Software Defined Everything

The implementation of technology is somewhat cyclical. We have matured from mainframe technology to ASP to cloud and now to software defined "everything" and convergence. Unfortunately, the technology trend seems to be a little confusing for many consumers. We must have automation with in our environments in order to be efficient. Automation is the ability to do processes without human interaction. Our ability to set, or better put, pre-set configurations, rules, and authority to execute specific tasks within our environment.

Development of the Virtual Machine:

The development of a virtual machine shares many traits with the development of a physical machine. We must load software to address the hardware, work through driver issues, and present an operating system so that the applications can perform the tasks we desire. This is a very manual process without automation. Although a virtual machine, and associated management software will provide a level of automation, software defined infrastructure is much more.

Building a Software Defined Infrastructure:

Prior to implementing a virtual machine within a software defined infrastructure, we would define process by which the virtual machine is configured. That process will include the hypervisor and the configuration of:

- storage
- network
- security
- software
- etc.

Upon completion, the virtual machine is 100% functional, ready to be used within the environment. All the storage, software, network, security and critical components are working together to provide an operating environment for immediate consumption.

3 Steps to a Software Defined Infrastructure

Step 1: Building a software defined infrastructure is not a rip and replace strategy. Building this level of automation is typically completed in phases, consider the following:

What level of automation are you currently using? Some ideas maybe:

- Backup and restore/geographically dispersed data replication
- Network and firewall infrastructure
- Storage area network and direct attached storage environment
- Computer environment with physical servers/virtual servers/blade servers
- Security, authorizations, and compliance
- Mobility access
- Operational management and accountability
- Custom applications built in house/applications purchased from a commercial vendor
- Database architecture

Now that we have defined some of the variables within our environment, we need to take a step back and ask: What level of automation currently exists?

Step 2: *is to understand* the automation used within our environments. For example: Developing a virtual machine has some automation, although is not necessarily a software defined infrastructure. Remember we are talking about infrastructure that performs tasks based on policy and process, automatically.

Step 3: *is about acting*. Once we have a good picture of what automation is in place, as well as the true definition of what automation

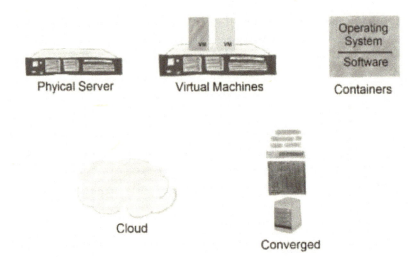

is, let's act and begin to build a software defined infrastructure. Within a software defined infrastructure, we want the ability to tie all of the components together. This will require some form of communication standard among all of the components, wherein the automation can occur (ie: API, ESB, RestFUL, etc...). A few technology examples include:

- **Converged systems**. A converged system should include all components that need to be automated: software, network, storage, visualization, operational strength, open standards and security. Once you place your solution within a converged solution, it should be a little slice of heaven... policy driven, repeatable and scalable. For your environment, a converged system may be a great fit for some of your business needs. If your environment has high turnover, perhaps is deployable, or looking to reduce/reallocate "specialized" technologists, converged solutions are great fit.
- **Cloud technology**. Cloud technology allows for the provisioning of all resources to automate the delivery of a specific technology service. Cloud and converged may

be similar conversations. The concept of "cloud" often implies that the solution is hosted "somewhere else", although many cloud architectures are somewhere between your local facility and the clouds.

Cloud technology, like converged, may be better understood as an automated infrastructure. The business objective is to increase repeatability while decreasing complexity. The number of specialized technologists within your environment should be decreasing year-over-year. The implementation of automation, like cloud and converged technologies, allow for compute services to be delivered in a predictable fashion, while maintaining consistency for environments that have little to no tolerance for change.

Step 3: Building Compute to meet your needs. There are several realities about the future of compute, to highlight two:

- **Mobile devices**: we live in an exciting time where the power of compute is within the palm of our hand. We continue to see the reduced communication on the computer bus to deliver common compute resources like CPU (central processing unit) and GPU (graphics processing unit). We see the reduction of the APU (accelerated processing unit) offered by AMD, similar merge processing units offered by Intel. The consolidation of processing chips allows for compute power as well as many other technologies, to fit in a smaller space.
- **Data Center Space**: the reality is that without the consolidation of the enterprise infrastructure, soon there will not be enough energy to provide the amount of compute that society requires. The future compute is to increase compute resources within considerably smaller spaces, at the same or reduced prices.

Storage and our Future

Understanding storage technologies and their functions is critical to building a robust, repeatable, scalable and cost stabilized solution. Too often, storage is consumed with little understanding of the functionality within the storage environment. This often translates to increased costs and missed expectations. Along with systems management and security, storage is a core pillar within a successful enterprise architecture. The storage demand for many environments represents a notable part of the information technology budget.

- What are the key technologies related to storage?
- What is the relevance of the key technologies to my business requirement?
- How does the technology enhance my security profile, authorization process?
- What is the impact to solutions like data analytics, cloud and others?

Many of our environments support multiple storage solutions. It is important to note that one-size does not always fit all business requirements. Flexibility and performance will continue to be critical success factors moving into the future.

Gather the Customer Requirements

GVL is looking for a more efficient way to manage their storage environment, and more importantly the unprecedented storage growth/demand for GVL consumers. GVL is reaching capacity and is interested in expanding their storage environment. GVL has heard about the rise of SSD/Flash technology and the decrease of spinning disk, and need to make sure they implement the proper storage foundation to meet varied business needs. Some of the details of the GVL environment today includes:

- 80% spinning disk to a storage area network.
- 68% transactional workloads (database, e-mail, applications) with high burst IOP requirements
- 32% file based workloads (archive, shared files)
- Minimal flash/SSD storage implemented today
- Over 65% virtualization in the environment
- Minimal desktop virtualization today, although is a future expectation
- Minimal analytics today, although aggressively assuming data analytic workload requests.

GVL is looking for the following storage foundation that should provide the following **functional requirements**:

- …support natively block, file and object storage via a native (minimum of 1-Gb/s) converged controller, not a bolt on module and/or blade.
- …support spinning disk (high performance and high capacity), SSD and Flash technology all within the same array.
- …be able to add new arrays in the future without having to re-harden the array. All arrays should share a common operating system to simplify security operations and reduce vulnerabilities.
- …guaranteed six 9's availability for the storage environment.
- …provide 5-year warranty on SSD technologies.
- …should provide a minimal footprint related to power and space through minimizing "array sprawl".
- …employ hardware acceleration for RAID, thin provisioning and storage processing infrastructure. Hardware acceleration should be native, not an add-on card.
- Storage should provide acquisition flexibility. For example: provide an OPEX and CAPEX model.

Functional Requirements and Business Requirements

Now that we have some of GVL functional requirements, we can begin to review applicable technologies. Critical to our success will be to understand some key technologies and how they apply to GVLs business requirements:

- Security is a critical concern for GVL. The fluid nature of attacks and the cost associated to build security controls and move through the authorization process are primary business drivers for GVL. Data is distributed geographically.
- Although analytics has been started in another department, GVL IT Department is confident that analytics will touch all areas of their business in the next one to three years. Our storage solution must be conducive with our future growth and support high performance data analytics.
- Storage growth with our current technology will force GVL into a data center expansion project. The growth of data is not

decreasing, we need to figure out how to get more storage capacity with less physical space.

Speaking the "Storage language" will reduce cost

Understanding the core technology for storage may assist in understanding the storage solutions provided by vendors. The lexicon will assist us in making more "educated" decisions related to storage. Storage represents a large cost in most organizations and will continue to do so in the years to follow. Understanding more about storage will allow all consumers to optimize performance and develop strategies to drive down operating expense. To meet the needs of GVL, the following technologies will have to be implemented/present as part of the storage architecture:

Solid State and Flash

- **Topic impact to my organization:** Availability, Data Loss, Performance, Cost. Solid State / Flash technology, coupled with a thin provisioned environment will dramatically reduce your storage cost, and increase performance.
- **Security / Authorization Impact**: Yes. Residual data can be found within non-RAM based solid state drive implementations. Traceability of the data, and destruction of the data will be required by most security controls.
- **Applicable Solution Impact:** Data Analytics, General Storage Use

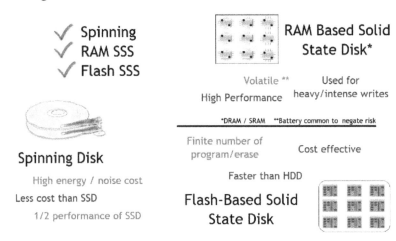

✓ Spinning
✓ RAM SSS
✓ Flash SSS

Spinning Disk

High energy / noise cost
Less cost than SSD
1/2 performance of SSD

RAM Based Solid State Disk*

Volatile **   Used for
High Performance   heavy/intense writes

*DRAM / SRAM   **Battery common to negate risk

Finite number of program/erase   Cost effective

Faster than HDD

Flash-Based Solid State Disk

- **Associated Terms**: SSD, EFDS, NAND, MLC, SLC, NVDIMM, Hyper Dimm, RAM, Flash, Volatile/Non-Volatile, Persistent Data, Solid State Storage (SSS)

Two terms that are often confused within the industry: Solid State and Flash. Solid State Drive (although there are no moving parts OR drive per se) is a non-spinning iSCSI target. Originally deployed as a collection of RAM, is now primarily using Flash technology or a hybrid between DRAM and Flash. Flash, perfected around the turn of the century is a component of a SSD. A common example of flash is a thumb drive.

- **When developing a solution, remember the following:**
  o SSD will leverage RAM, Flash or a hybrid approach.
  o RAM is typically volatile. Basically: Power loss of the device will create data loss. This can be circumvented with the addition of batteries and write technology to non-volatile space.
  o RAM (SDRAM) although volatile is very fast.
  o Flash is non-volatile. When power is lost, data is retained.
  o Hybrid RAM+Flash (often call NVDIMM / Hyper Dimm) will use RAM for performance, and upon system failure, write the data to flash to have zero data loss.

Sub-LUN Tiering

- **Impact to my organization:** Performance, Cost. Tiering data will provide you with an optimal storage environment reducing power, space, and cost, while increase utilization from a standard 40% to 85+%.
- **Security / Authorization Impact**: Yes. Policy on how the data is tiered will impact the security baseline. If the security baseline requires data to be on a specific LUN, no problem, the efficiency of the tiering architecture will be diminished greatly.

- **Associated Terms**: Data Management, Automated Tiered Storage Management (ATS), sub-volume based storage, data locking, adaptive optimization.

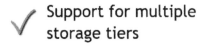 Support for multiple storage tiers

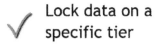 Lock data on a specific tier

✓ Tiering block size and schedule

Sub-LUN Tiering is the ability to move data within the array automatically. The functionality exists with several vendors. Tiering leverages storage virtualization pools and allows data to be moved between the pools. Metadata is collected and analyzed to execute tiering policies. Typically leveraged to maximize available storage resources. Place the data type to a specific section of the storage array.

- **When developing a solution, remember the following:**
    - Require a minimum of three tiers? Do the number of tiers vary dependent upon the disk type? (ie: SATA, SSD…). **Why?** This may impact your decision to purchase an array that supports multiple storage media (SATA, SSD, etc..) which will ultimately drive down cost and increase performance.
    - Tiering leverages storage resources: hardware acceleration is an important performance variable.
    - Can dynamic policy changes be made? **Why?** Policies govern the actions of the tiering. You may need the ability to change policy to align with your business.
    - Can you lock data on a specific tier? **Why?** Some applications may not allow the data to be tiered.
    - Can you adjust the level of automated tiering based on specific applications, environments? **Why?** Application performance may dictate different values.
    - Does the solution support tiering of snapshot data?
    - Is auto-tuning available to meet SLAs?

- o Is there a software cost for tiering?
- o Key to sub-LUN tiering is cost savings, ultimately shifting workload data to less expensive SATA drives from performance based SSD.
- o Pre-planning is critical to success with developing the correct policies that will drive the tiering activities.
- o What is the block size that is migrated to the next tier? (128MB, 512KB…) **Why?** Block size has a direct impact on cost and performance.
- o What is the tiering schedule (every 30 min, 24 hours)? Can the schedule for customized?
- o Does tiering create unacceptable latencies that only SSD volumes can overcome?

Thin In-Line Deduplication

- **Impact to my organization:** Operational Cost, Performance. Deduplication will reduce the actual storage needed within your environment, saving you money while establishing a performance focus environment.
- **Security / Authorization Impact**: Minimal. Deduplicated data will become part of the security baseline artifacts. You will have to establish a location to re-hydrate the de-duplicated data as needed.
- **Associated Terms**: Thin Persistence, Thin Reclamation, Zero Block Deduplication, Hardware Accelerated Deduplication, ASIC

Non-wide striping LUN (traditional)

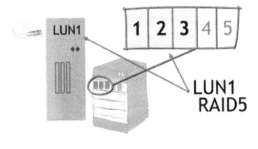

Wide-striping LUN

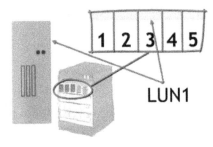

To truly understand storage functionality, and certainly deduplication, it is important to understand the difference between non-wide striping LUNs and system wide-striping LUNs.

A **non-wide striping LUN** is defined over several physical drives. The number of drives that can participate in a LUN, as well as the drive types, is dependent upon the storage array.

The **wide-striping LUN** allows the LUN to leverage drives throughout the array. The IOPs associated with a LUN is directly tied to the number of hard drives, often called spindles, which are working to satisfy the request. In a wide-striping LUN configuration, you have small amounts of data being served by many "spindles", the result is performance.

Think back to a time you have either moved yourself or assisted someone else with a move. If you are working by yourself, taking a single box from the house and placing it in the back of the moving van, your efforts will take some time. Now imagine having 400 of your close friends come over to assist, the move will go very fast. This is the difference between system wide striping and non-wide striping.

Now that we understand LUNs, let's talk about deduplication. Deduplication of storage data has a direct impact on storage capacity. Flash technology utilization to cost ratio is more attractive when leveraging technology that can eliminate "data redundancy" in your environment. In a virtual environment, there is a high degree of data redundancy, which can create a compute intense environment, highlighting the need for deduplication technologies. Software based deduplication or external (to the storage array) appliance-based deduplication will not produce the same results as a storage infrastructure with integrated hardware acceleration for deduplication tasks.

- **When developing a solution, remember the following:**
  - o Thin inline deduplication should not require pre-planning or up-front space reservations.
  - o Storage solutions should support system-wide striping simultaneously allows high disk utilization and performance.
  - o Thin Deduplication software should deliver inline, block-level deduplication minimizing performance impact by leveraging ASIC and/or capacity inefficiency tradeoffs
  - o Solution should include built-in, zero reclaim mechanism to drive efficient inline zero block deduplication at the hardware layer
  - o Hardware-accelerated "fat-to-thin" volume conversions
  - o Reclamation reclaims unneeded space from snapshots and remote copies
  - o Hardware offload engines for identifying duplicated data
  - o Fast lookup tables that store location pointers to accelerate data access
  - o Tri-layer addresses translation mechanism akin to Virtual Memory lookup tables

Flat Backup

- **Impact to my organization:** Cost, Performance
- **Security / Authorization Impact**: Backup process is part of a security baseline. Many security policies require a secondary copy of all virtual machines. Flat backup is an inexpensive alternative to accomplish this for large number of virtual systems.

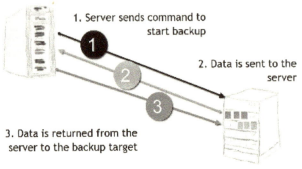

1. Server sends command to start backup

2. Data is sent to the server

3. Data is returned from the server to the backup target

Traditional Backup

- **Applicable Solution:** VMware vSphere environments
- **Associated Terms**: Agentless backup, Block Backup, VSS, LUN Backup

Certainly, a dream of all IT administrators is the ability to backup data without backup software. Flat backup is the ability to back up a LUN directly to the storage array. Software is loaded to associate the data with the storage infrastructure, and LUN based backup and recovery is possible, without backup software.

- **When developing a solution, remember the following:**
  - o Flat Backup is LUN based. Everything in the LUN will be backed up.
  - o Individual file recovery is not available. The LUN can be restored to a "temp" machine where individual file recovery may be accomplished.
  - o Flat backup is very fast as it avoids the transport through the server and storage infrastructure to accomplish a backup.
  - o Following a successful backup, incremental backups are performed on the LUN to provide additional performance gains.

Zero-Reclamation

- **Impact to my organization:** Cost
- **Security / Authorization Impact**: Minimal.
- **Applicable Solution Impact:** Thin Provisioned Environments, Virtualized environments

- **Associated Terms**: zero-fill, zero reclaim, SCSI unmap, thin provisioned virtual volumes (TPVVs),

A spinning disk can overwrite data directly on the drive in any sector. The hard drive firmware may swap damaged blocks with spare areas, although as a result bits and pieces are often still present. Traditionally, when data is deleted on a physical host, the OS reports that space has been freed, but the storage array is not informed that the data is no longer in use. For example: "when VMs are deleted or migrated from a TPVV (thin provisioned virtual volume), vCenter reports available storage space on the volume but the blocks for the deleted or moved VMs and files remain allocated at the storage level, resulting in over-provisioning".

Thin technology is state-of-the-art, and its inline zero-reclaim and selectable dedupe should be accelerated by a custom ASIC. Many storage vendors place all functions on the storage CPU which greatly impacts performance. When deleting snapshots, capacity should be returned to the CPG (Common Provisioning Group) automatically.

- **When developing a solution, remember the following:**
  - ASIC chip for zero-reclamation allows the storage CPU to focus on other performance tasks.

Downstream Snapshot Recovery

- **Impact to my organization:** Cost, Performance, Loss of Data
- **Security / Authorization Impact**: Direct challenge related to recoverability of "snapshot" data will impact a security baseline.
- **Applicable Solution Impact:** All environments running snapshots of data
- **Associated Terms**: Snapshot, Storage foundation point, point in time copy

Snapshots are a space efficient, point in time image of an application. Commonly used for quick and reliable recovery operations. Once a snapshot is taken, the next snapshot only captures "updates" to the previous snapshot. Snapshot technology is used by many storage vendors, although if the snapshot cannot retrieve "downstream" snapshots, the utility of the service is great compromised. A "downstream" snapshot example: GVL has an application that has snapshots taken at 0600, 1130, 1430, 1830 and 2230 every day. The GVL administrator notices an anomaly with the GVL application, and work on the cause and solution consumes most of the day. By 1530 the GVL administrator has a solution, although will need to validate assumptions on captured snapshots. The GVL administrator restores snapshots from 0600, 1130 and 1430 to validate the solution. Be careful, some vendors only capture a single snapshot and then re-write the snapshot. Had this been the configuration of the GVL environment, it may have been very difficult to understand the root of the anomaly.

- **When developing a solution, remember the following:**
  - o Snapshots should allow for you to recover more than that most recent snapshot and more than one snapshot. This is referred to as "downstream recovery" where you can restore a snapshot taken, for example, three snapshots in the past.
  - o Recovery of a snapshot should not invalidate other snapshots already captured.
  - o Can you configure the number of snapshots that are retained? **Why?** Recovery alternatives.
  - o A default capacity reservation on your storage environment is 20% for snapshot recovery. The percentage can be adjusted based on your environment, number of snapshots and business requirements.

Reservationless Storage

- **Impact to my organization:** Cost, Performance, Loss of Data
- **Security / Authorization Impact**: Minimal. Operational impact.
- **Applicable Solution Impact:** All storage solutions

Some storage arrays allow "reservationless" storage. You don't have to reserve snapshot capacity that you may not ever need, you don't have to create special pools of disk drives that are only used for thin provisioning and best of all you don't have to pay for professional capacity planning services that you end up changing at a later time.

- **When developing a solution, remember the following:**

- A reservationless environment allows the you to have a flexible environment
- Save time and effort with reservationless storage.

Flash Cache

- **Impact to my organization:** Cost, Performance
- **Security / Authorization Impact**: Limited impact.
- **Applicable Solution Impact:** All solutions
- **Associated Terms**: Cache, Express Writes

Flash Cache accelerates random reads by extending the storage system cache by using SSD capacity and can be applied selectively or across the array. SSDs can be dedicated to this role or segmented for use in both typical tiering duty and as part of the cache extension. This feature means cold reads find their way into the cache more quickly, potentially doubling random read rates from disk and reducing read latency by up to 70%.

- **When developing a solution, remember the following:**
  - Does your storage allow concurrent use of Flash Cache and sub-LUN tiering and regular SSD volumes? Concurrent use will enable cost savings and higher performance across the array.
  - To help address write latency, how does the storage solution address efficiencies designed for database workloads that better handle transactional logs?
  - Build a storage solution that allows you to add to your HDD-based system, add a small number of SSDs and give the arrays a vastly improved performance profile with these new features without making any other changes or large investments in new hardware.
  - Build a storage solution for a repeat read environment with SSDs for Flash Cache and Nearline HDDs for the primary storage.

Thin / Fat Provisioning

- **Impact to my organization:** Cost

- **Security / Authorization Impact**: Thin provisioning as a technology has no specific authorization/security impact, although the security baseline will require "traceability" of the data within the thin environment. (see Sub-LUN Tiering – Data Locking)
- **Applicable Solution Impact:** Storage in general
- **Associated Terms**: TP, FP, Thin Provisioning, Fat Provisioning, Thin Arrays, Thin LUNs, Oversubscription, Overallocation

Fat provisioning takes into consideration the current and projected storage utilization for a user/application and allocates the storage accordingly. As a result, fat provisioning historically has a low

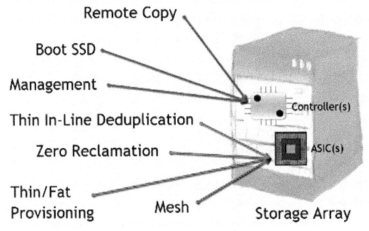

utilization percentage, driving up storage cost. For example: GVL requires 100TB today, although over the next 3 years is projected to use 200TB. 300TB is allocated to the LUN in support of the user, with the acknowledgement that storage utilization will be minimal. On average, fast provisioning utilization is approximately 40%, wasting 60% of storage.

Thin provisioning operates by allocating disk capacity in a flexible manner among multiple users, based on the minimum space required by each user at any given time. Storage consumption is managed, and capacity is typically added when the array is at 70-80% utilized. It is not uncommon for consumers to have 90-98% storage utilization in a thin provisioned environment. Added thin provisioning benefits include reduced consumption of electrical energy, smaller hardware space requirements and reduced heat generation compared with traditional fat provisioned storage systems.

- **When developing a solution, remember the following:**
  - o Fat Provisioning typically has low utilization percentages resulting in wasted storage capacity / cost.
  - o Thin Provisioning allocates storage in a flexible manner, based on minimum storage space required by the user.
  - o Thin provisioning automates and simplifies the LUN provisioning process through automation and user defined policy/process. The automated LUN provisioning requires resources from the storage array. For optimal performance, seek a thin provisioning storage array that has hardware accelerated thin provisioning VS software based thin provisioning. The performance impact will become more apparent as you increase utilization of the storage array. The ASIC hardware accelerated chip makes a notable difference.
  - o Capacity management is critical in a thin provisioned environment. Applications will fail if storage is not available to fulfill the thin provisioned environment. Manage the thin provisioned environment to 75% utilized, then order more capacity.
  - o An online connection to the storage vendors data base helps accurately monitor storage utilization.

Data Compression

- **Impact to my organization:** Cost, Performance
- **Security / Authorization Impact**: Minimal
- **Applicable Solution Impact:** Storage in general
- **Associated Terms**: Array Overhead

Data compression can be categorized into two basic strategies: lossy and lossless. Both perform compression activities, and the effectiveness is dependent upon the implementation of the compression strategy.

Lossless leverages "a model/predictive" and a "coder". Basically, a coder assigns shorter codes based on "probability model" of the commonality of the character. For example: the Morse Code codes the alphabet into a series of dots and dashes. Common letters like A, E, I, T in Morse Code have the smallest codes, as they are more frequently used. **Lossy** compression removes unneeded characters. For example: a graphic file that has unimportant data that is not seen by the eye.

Data compression is available in a simple form on your desktop, laptop or tablet. Although many consumers seek more efficient forms of storage management via a superior cost structure and more efficient array overhead.

- **When developing a solution, remember the following:**
  - Define the type of compression that is best suited to meet business needs.
  - Understand the performance impact of data compression.
  - Understand the impact of data compression as it relates to interconnected technologies like thin provisioning, snapshots, deduplication and virtualization
  - Compare total cost of ownership leveraging compression vs efficient array overhead.

Block, File, Object Storage

- **Impact to my organization:** Cost, Performance, Scalability
- **Security / Authorization Impact**: Minimal
- **Applicable Solution Impact:** Storage in general
- **Associated Terms**: Storage Area Network (SAN), Network Attached Storage (NAS), Direct Attached Storage (DAS), NFS, Solid State Drives (SSD), Hard Disk Drives (HDD)

We build a storage environment to satisfy a business need. We may have a transactional environment that requires rapid read and write activity, a file environment that may write a file once and read multiple times, direct read and write activity via http calls like put and get and/or an archival location where files are written once for long term storage. We may have business needs that require a hybrid of storage technology, for example: 20% requires transactional support whereas 60% can be stored on disk that is focused on capacity, and 20% supports direct http calls.

In the complex business environment of today, rarely will one size fit all storage needs. Some vendors may imply that their storage defies the nature of disk types and performance, although in the 30+ years I

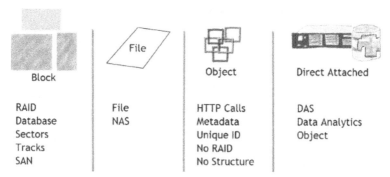

Block	File	Object	Direct Attached
RAID	File	HTTP Calls	DAS
Database	NAS	Metadata	Data Analytics
Sectors		Unique ID	Object
Tracks		No RAID	
SAN		No Structure	

have been in the industry...I have yet to find that vendor.

The storage array needs to be capable of supporting diverse business workloads, while providing flexibility for HDD to SSD to Block to File to Object storage solutions. Couple the technology with an enhanced security posture and you have a cost effective and secure storage infrastructure. The storage arrays should be configured with the same operating system, no matter the number of drives and/or the type of drives the array will support: hence greatly increasing your security profile and saving you operational cost.

- **When developing a solution, remember the following:**
  - o Storage is not one size fits all. Storage must be flexible to meet customer needs.
  - o Storage should be intelligent allowing for all types SSD, HDD, Block, File, and Object.
  - o Storage array controller should be a consistent operating system for all storage arrays providing enhanced security and cost savings.
  - o Storage should have both a CAPEX and OPEX financial model.

Finding the correct storage solution

Multiple storage solutions from converged storage to network attached to storage area network to direct / attached are designed to support multiple business requirements. Some of the key attributes should include:

- Storage solutions to extend functionality of your existing storage environment.
- Storage providing performance and flexibility with array environments that support:
  - Same operating system across array heads providing an organization with significant cost savings related to security, hardening, operations and sustainability.
  - Thin provisioning and policy-based disk management allowing for storage workloads to automatically move from disk type to recognize maximum disk utilization and cost savings.
  - Hardware accelerated storage operations that leverage the ASIC chip, providing maximum performance while offloading processing task from the storage processors.
- Storage solutions that support security requirements:
  - FIPS 140-2
  - DoD STIG

Ask yourself, "How does this information assist me in making the right decisions related to storage"? The most effective strategy is to align our business requirement with the functionality of the technology. To help us get started, we have provided a weighted evaluation:

Putting it all together | Weighted Evaluation

The weighted evaluation looks at two areas: **native** functionality and the **relevance** of the functional requirements to meet your business requirements. An example from GVL will need to complete the spreadsheet to match the requirements of their environment.

Weighted Evaluation to *Align objectives to tool functionality:* To gather the real opinion of an organization, distribute the evaluation independently to each team member in a non-collaborative approach. Collect the information from the evaluation, then compare and contrast. If needed, bring the team together to discuss the results. This approach allows an organization to be more functional focused rather than product focused.

Note that the numeric value is dictated by the individual completing the evaluation, it does not always represent functionality of the actual storage, but rather the individuals understanding of the functionality of the storage. Leveraging the evaluation tool, or another process within your organization is strongly suggested. The evaluation will provide a level playing field for all related technologies and decision variables that are critical to a cost-effective conclusion.

Evaluation
preferred score is 10

Objective	Native (0-10)	Relevant (0-10)
Support SSD, FLASH, HDD on same array controller.	10	10
Support for block, file and object environments	10	10
Snapshots should allow for recovery of multiple restoration snapshots, not limited to the most current snapshot. Often referred to as "downstream recovery".	10	10
Support for object storage in the same array controller.	10	10
Storage workloads support automated workflow based on storage need and use.	10	10

Storage:

Weighted Values	Actual	Possible
Native	200	200
Relevance	200	200

	Actual	Possible
Overall Score	400	400
Desirable Percentage*		100%

Market Research – Functional Requirements

To help you get started we must summarize some functional requirements that will assist in your selection of a storage infrastructure. The list is not all inclusive, although should be a good start:

- Solution must support SSD, FLASH, HDD on same array controller.

- Solution must provide support for block, file and object environments.
- Solution should provide snapshots that allow for recovery of multiple restoration snapshots, not limited to the most current snapshot. Often referred to as "downstream recovery".
- Storage workloads must support automated workflow based on storage need and historical usage patterns.
- Battery backup and automated data movement for DRAM/SRAM SSD must be a default standard for all SSD technologies.
- Solution must provide a minimum of SSD extended warranty for 5 years.
- Solution must support a minimum of 3 tiers for sub-lun tiering.
- It is preferred that sub-lun tiering is supported by an internal card in addition to the storage processor(s).
- Solution must support automated tiering based on applications needs and agency defined policy.
- Solution tiering must support snapshot data.
- Preference will be given to solutions that provide minimal latency impact for tiering operations based on a workload provided by the organization.
- Solution must support inline deduplication.
- Inline deduplication should not require up-front space reservations.
- Preference will be given to integrated native zero reclamation hardware (not an add-on software).
- Solution must reclaim unneeded space from snapshots and remote copies.
- Deduplication must support fast lookup tables and store location pointers to accelerate data access.
- Solution must support LUN / block backup without having to travel to the server for instruction.
- Storage must allow concurrent use of adaptive flash cache and adaptive optimization sub-tiering.

- Storage must support a wide range of business requirements from transactional databases to log files on the same storage array.
- Storage solution should offer both CAPEX and OPEX acquisition models.

Chapter 3: Automated Technology

Our ability to access information has dramatically changed over the past five years. We have truly entered an anytime/anywhere computing model. Anytime/anywhere computing is dependent upon a well-executed system management strategy, and a robust and consistent core infrastructure. Now that we've established these two primary IT pillars, what is our strategy to provide access to services (i.e. file sharing, email, applications)? There are several delivery models available:

Automated Infrastructure Delivery

An automated infrastructure can be delivered as cloud services or converged architecture. The primary objective of this delivery model is to automate as much of the delivery of technology as possible. An automated infrastructure can be found within our firewall, or external as a public offering. Many of the technologies discussed within systems management and core infrastructure are carefully orchestrated to provide an automated delivery of IT resources.

And automated infrastructure primarily performs the following functions:

- service catalog
- provision
- orchestration
- policy/rule-based computing
- software defined infrastructure

Hardware and/or software provide the automated infrastructure, as well as services to implement, training and sustainment of the environment as needed.

Cloud Delivery

Cloud technology is changing our lives. Illustrated below are a few examples of how this amazing technology is already impacting both our personal lives as well as our business lives. Some examples of cloud technology include:

- Delivery of medical benefits, images and services
- Submission of tax returns and collection of information related to taxes

- University research projects and support of federal agencies
- Collection and sharing of law enforcement data, profiles and surveillance

We have multiple cloud solutions, such as private, multi-tenant and hybrid delivery models. For many organizations, placing their data and services within a multi-tenant "shared environment" simply goes against the organization's business rules. While multi-tenant technology has the potential of saving money and simplifying your IT life, many organizations simply are not ready since often it requires them to change the way they operate. Too often cloud services bring us back to the days when technology attempted to dictate business need, a model that simply does not have to be.

As we address information technology requirements, restricted budgets, and condensed timelines; many of the core information technology components are simple "skipped" within IT solutions. Whether the restriction is time or money, often components like help desk, disaster recovery and/or service level agreement management may not be fully integrated into the solution.

Is a Dedicated/Private Cloud really a Cloud? The answer is yes, and here is why:

Cloud Automation

Many years ago, we implemented mainframe technologies with virtualization as a core component, and automated workflow within the virtual environment was an absolute. During the 1980s, as x86 servers became more prevalent, the common configuration was a physical server, and dictated by the critical nature of the service, many servers were configured in a cluster. As we moved into the 1990s and now the 2000s, virtualization has consolidated many of our physical servers, although we quickly discovered that virtualization without automation was simply more servers that we had to manage.

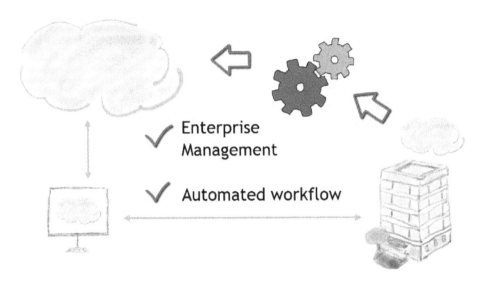

Enterprise Management

Automated workflow

A cloud infrastructure, by default, runs within a virtual environment. Coupled with the virtual environment is workflow automation. Virtualization, automation, and workflow are common components of what is often referred to as cloud orchestration. One of the byproducts associated with cloud automation is the ability to provision resources.

Many organizations have defined process by which new enterprise resources are made available within their network. The defined process often includes an analysis of available budget, adequate ports, cooling, rack space and many other variables that will ultimately impact the success of a new information technology service. Within many Cloud solutions, many if not all the workflow process can be automated as part of the cloud orchestration/provisioning activities. Many of the data points required to make an informed decision about adding new resources, are available somewhere within the cloud environment. The ability to automate workflow, virtualization and automated provisioning is one of many benefits achieved with a private or multitenant cloud infrastructure.

Cloud Operations

Before continuing, ask yourself this simple question, "How organized are you?" Many of us would not agree that being organized directly translates to being more efficient. Although many of us understand this to be true, often we find ourselves less organized then we would like to be. Operational support for our information technology environments too often shares the same fate as our organizational efforts.

Operational support includes change management, configuration management, incident management, and many of the processes and philosophy that enables successful operational environments. Cloud technology that is compliant with current security policies and controls must have well defined configuration management disciplines. In fact, satisfying many of the controls require a detailed "mapping" of the impact a specific action will take within the cloud, as well as all of the touch points for that action, coupled with the impact to the configuration of the cloud environment.

Cloud Reporting

Reporting often includes many facets of the information technology environment, operation, statistical usage, predictive foresight, log aggregation, and many other valuable data points to manage our environment. Within a cloud environment, all these data points, as well as others are used to manage the cloud experience.

Terms like cloud metering, chargeback and show back. All these terms leverage reporting components designed to optimize your cloud experience. Some benefits associated with cloud reporting include, although are not limited to:

Time and Energy: cloud technologies require a dedicated metric for usage with in the cloud environment. Whether your organization absorbs these costs directly, or sub organizations contribute to meeting these financial responsibilities.

Cloud Metering: many cloud infrastructures allow the assignment and cost collection to core components with in the computing environment which include: storage capacity, processing and memory utilization.

Application costs: understanding the core costs associated with the cloud infrastructure is important, although most of the services provided within a cloud are dependent upon applications (i.e.: email, file sharing, organizational applications).

Cloud Security

Security is often why consumers are hesitant to adopt cloud. Cloud security is critical, within a multi-tenant as well as a private cloud environment. Why should you trust the cloud? Consider the following:

If I were to purchase a home in the middle of a thriving metropolis, I would have a heightened awareness of my surroundings, perhaps home alarms, deadbolts, and other security measures, assuming that a break in will occur. If I purchased a home in the middle of the country, I may leave the house unlocked, as the probability is very low that anyone would want to break in to my home.

Environments that are public facing often have enhanced security practices simply because probability is high. Whereas, for many years, security found within an organization information technology environment were inconsistent, simply because probability of a security breach is perceived to be less.

Let's translate this into cloud technology. Whether you have decided to leverage a multitenant or a dedicated/private cloud, the security used to build the cloud is consistent and capable of handling both "living in the city (multi-tenant) and living in the country (dedicated/private)". Cloud technology always assumes that the probability of a security breach is extremely high, hence many security practices are implemented that may not be seen within an isolated infrastructure environment serving an organization.

Mobility

The delivery of technology is dependent upon an automated/cloud structure, although equally important is how the

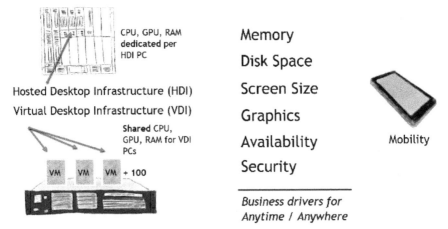

data and services are consumed. In today's world, consumption of data often includes remote and local access. Many organizations defined this as the difference between a desktop within the facility and the "take anywhere" mobile device. The definition certainly has merit, although the reality is consumption of data may lead to a mobile device within the facility firewall, or in a forward deployed location, hence the line becomes very distorted. Often decisions for data/services consumption can be based upon the following:

- Memory: how much memory is needed to run the application?
- Disk space: how much disk space is required to run the application?
- Screen size: does the screen size impact the functionality of the application? A great example: try to look at the spreadsheet on a smart phone.
- Graphics: what is needed to run the application?
- Availability: does the location require consistent connectivity to the data source? May the consumer use the application in an off-line configuration? Availability directly correlates to disk space if used in an off-line configuration.
- Security: what level of security is required? Does the security level required separation of personal and work data/applications? Can the device perform decryption and encryption processes? What happens if the device becomes lost?

Connectivity to devices of the future will continue to evolve our enterprise architecture from wired to wireless technology. Wireless implementations by default provide accurate inventory, policy based

Wireless Strategy

☐ Security
  Suite B
☐ Operational
  Policies
  Automation
☐ Simplify
  No de-Crypt at AP

Does not de-crypt at Access Point

Relieve load from Access Point to Controller

Access Point

Controller

AES 256 Suite B

Encryption WIDS Firewall

✓ Policy / Rules Based

FIPS 140-2 Certified

✓ Automated Workflow

Device

Operational Security

✓ Mobile device on-boarding

on boarding, and automation.

Wireless technology allows a network infrastructure to inspect both the identity and device of the consumer, and quarantine as necessary. Once granted access, the behavior of the consumer can be monitored and modified based upon predefined policy.

Virtual and Hosted Desktop Infrastructure

Virtual desktop environments provide consistency for the deployment and management of desktop environments. Both virtual

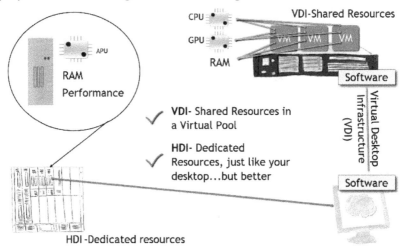

desktop (VDI) as well as hosted desktop infrastructure (HDI) are options for users of the infrastructure. The objective of both VDI and HDI is to automate the delivery of services provided by the enterprise infrastructure. Devices (tablets, smartphones, laptop, desktop) require access to the following:

- CPU (central processing unit)
- GPU (graphics processing unit)
- Disk Capacity
- RAM

Virtual Desktop Infrastructure (i.e.: remote desktop, Citirx) (VDI) provides access to shared resources within the enterprise architecture, primarily the server. Multiple consumers/devices connect to a virtual pool of resources, sharing those resources. Multiple virtual desktops are often installed on a single server. Connectivity to the shared resources is accomplished virtually. Hosted desktop infrastructure is also consumed virtually, although varies from a virtual desktop infrastructure as all resources are dedicated to a specific consumer.

Building a functional delivery strategy

There are too many variables to list, although the following are some key considerations when considering an enterprise architecture and delivery strategy:

Availability

- What services do you currently run in your environment that are targeted for an automated infrastructure?
- Of these services, which service(s) cannot be unavailable for more than five minutes?
- Of these services, which service(s) can be on available for up to 30 minutes?

Answer: If we are running an application at our local facility that can recover within five minutes, automated infrastructure should provide the same level of resilience. For example: Just because our

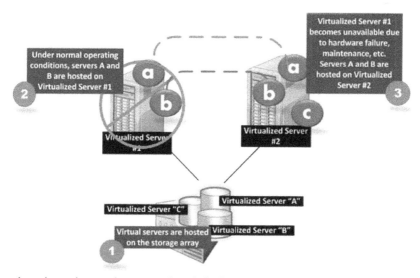

service is migrated to a cloud infrastructure does not negate the responsibility of information technology to provide performance and functionality?

As previously introduced: A service is defined as a functional result of the compute environment. The question that needs to be answered is, "How long can we be without this service?" In other words, "What is the impact to our organization if email is not available for five minutes, 30 minutes or four hours?"

Why is this important? At the root of all the technology, many decision-makers simply want to know the cost associated with maintaining a service. While many users may think all services are critical, after careful review and consideration, it becomes important to distinguish the impact of which services will be recovered within 5 minutes, while others are recovered within 4 hours, and still others are rarely, if ever, unavailable. When designing an enterprise architecture, all variables should be considered. Illustrated below is an example of failover between multiple sites. What will be your strategy?

Physical or Virtual

Does the application currently run in a hypervisor, or is it running on a physical server? If the application is currently not running in a hypervisor, has the application been validated to function in a virtual environment? What is the operating system?

Why is this important? If your applications are currently running within a hypervisor, your probability for success to a cloud increases considerably. If the application is not running within a hypervisor today, an automated infrastructure may be the best alternative.

Application Dependencies

What are the dependencies of the application? For example: Is there a database server or a set of front-end servers?

Why is this important? Too often, we forget about the dependencies and all the inner related services that allow that application to function properly. For some of our environments, discovering these dependencies can be a real challenge. Application dependencies will be important when choosing an automated infrastructure VS a cloud infrastructure, as success is often limited if the presentation of the application is in a cloud and the data structure to support the cloud is geo-graphical dispersed.

Storage Type

What is the storage requirement? Block, file, object?

Why is this important? The type of storage is very important when you begin to look at infrastructure architecture. You do not want to purchase a solution that only supports block-based storage when your application uses object-based storage. Remember, specific performance for your application is often directly tied to the storage. HP provides a wide array of storage alternatives.

Application Latency

What is the tolerated latency of the applications within the automated infrastructure? (i.e. latency between the presentation and data structure of the application).

Why is this important? Application latency between components can be the difference between a functional application on the cloud and one that does not work well. Remember that the application has certain tolerance levels for the data and presentation layers.

Location

- What is the target location for your enterprise infrastructure?
- Will some of the services be local, while other will reside in a geo-dispersed environment?
- Do you require a dedicated network circuit, or can you share?
- Does the network circuit need to be NIPR or SIPR?

Why is this important? The location of your servers and data will define the type of automated infrastructure that can be leveraged. Often this decision is closely correlated to security requirements. Network bandwidth will be a cost burden that grows as you expand your functionality. Make sure that you have multiple circuits at your hosting facility. Remember, the more network providers that are within a facility (i.e. AT&T, Sprint, L3, etc), the lower the connectivity price.

Functional Use

What will the automated infrastructure be used to deliver?
- Will the environment be hosting high-performance transactional data structures?
- Will the environment be primarily used for the dissemination/sharing of information?
- Will the architecture be used as a replication/backup target?

- How many CPUs and RAM does your application use today? What is the current utilization of those server resources in your physical environment today (broken out by servers, if possible)?
- An alternative answer to the questions is to define the virtual machines you would like to have available on the cloud. For example: VM1: 1 vCPU, 2GB RAM, 100GB storage; VM2: 4vCPU, 8GB RAM, 1TB storage, etc. Be sure to list the quantity of each virtual machine you are looking for. For example: 22 VM1, 12 VM2.

Why is this important? Cloud resources are often calculated based on the vCPU, not the virtual machine. Remember that a virtual machine is made up of multiple compute resources (processor, ram, storage). You need to define the makeup of your virtual machines; if not, it would be like purchasing a 'physical server' for file sharing and ending up with a 16-core / 800 GB RAM / 4 Pb server. Be specific about your needs and allow the infrastructure to meet the requirements.

Chapter 4: Security

Security plays a critical role within an enterprise architecture. Based upon your organization, security standards may range dramatically. Organizations often require security, implementation of

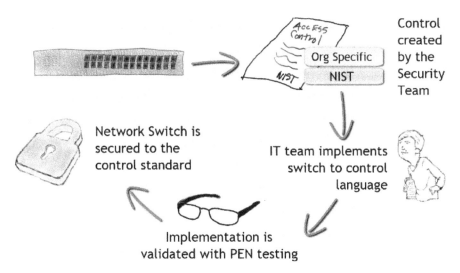

Control created by the Security Team

Network Switch is secured to the control standard

IT team implements switch to control language

Implementation is validated with PEN testing

standards, all managed through a security. Security authorizations include process, people and the technology. Configuration management, the core infrastructure and delivery of the service must all be considered when developing a security strategy.

Security Baseline

For many organizations, implementation of security is a team effort. The information technology team receives a piece of equipment, for example, a switch. The information technology team goes to the security team and solicits the security control(s) that need to be implemented on the switch. The controls govern the configuration of the switch (from a security perspective), often referred to as "hardening" is completed by the information technology team. Once the switch has been "hardened", it is often passed to the PEN testers. The PEN testers will test for vulnerabilities, often referred to as the "PEN Test". Once all these processes have been completed successfully, the network switch is secure and ready for operation. We have simply highlighted one component of the "system/service" that will require security. A standard "system/service (i.e: Email)" may require hundreds of components (process, software, hardware) to be secure, in a consistent manner.

Certification to Standards

Certifications for specific hardware, software and process are subcomponents of the security baseline and policy process. For the most part, certifications enable an organization to adopt a certified

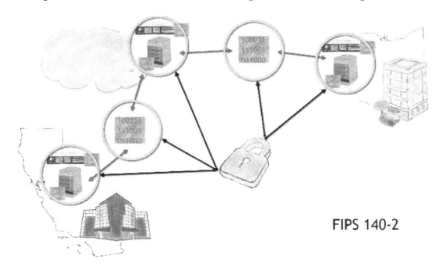

FIPS 140-2

standard, streamlining their agencies effort to provide a security baseline. It is not uncommon for certifications, like FIPS 140-2 to become a standard for data encryption.

As an example, FIPS 140-2 focuses on encryption standards for data at rest and a flight. The standard includes multiple levels and can take several months to receive final certification. Some devices impacted by FIPS 140-2 are servers, storage, desktops, laptops, mobile devices.

Used within the Department of Defense, it is not uncommon to see Security Technical Implementation Guides (STIGs) used as a baseline certification/standard for building enterprise architecture.

Security policy for an Enterprise Architecture?

The development of security controls, management of the security baseline and policy environment, as well as certification standards will have a direct impact on operating expense. Dependent upon the control; development, implementation, and hardening can cost an organization tens of thousands of dollars per control. Acquiring technologies that have already been certified, or successfully participate in a security baseline will greatly reduce operating expense and accelerate time required to make the service available to consumers.

Security Boundaries

A security boundary is a set of predefined process, software, and hardware that can be used as a core enterprise foundation. Systems management, core infrastructure, and delivery of information to consumers often make up a security boundary. Typically, the security boundary is focused on a specific deliverable (for example: internal applications, email, file sharing, etc.). Many agencies have begun to develop a core security boundary by which additional services can be added to that boundary. For example: an organization establishes systems management, core infrastructure and the delivery strategy, all protected by security standards and controls, and offer the infrastructure boundary to all new applications. Within their organization, as new applications/services are introduced, they will simply become an addendum to the original security boundary. This often does not alleviate the need to recertify the security baseline, although will greatly simplify the security process if you can build upon a consistent, and repeatable infrastructure.

Security Information and Event Management (SIEM)

Security events are generated from much of the infrastructure. These events are often "logged" into an event log. Event logs can hold

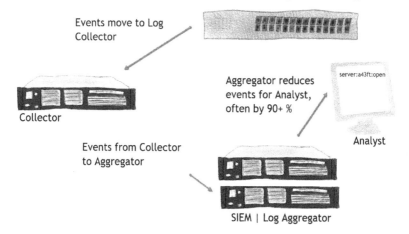

millions of events. Remember we are collecting events from all components (servers, storage, switches, etc..) of the system/service that we are providing (i.e.: email, internal applications, file sharing).

Let's use a network switch as an example. The network switch is a primary component of the enterprise architecture. The switch may generate thousands of events per day. For this example, let's assume that a collector (a software application running in the enterprise) is collecting and organizing all the events from the switch. The event collector then forwards the information to a log aggregator. The log aggregator is collecting similar event logs from collectors that are managing storage, servers, physical security, etc. Based upon policies, the log aggregator, often referred to as a SIEM, disposes of the "noise" or non-relevant events, and presents the analyst with actionable events for a deeper review and remediation.

Why is this important to the construction of an enterprise architecture? Security management is critical to the success of all services provided by the enterprise architecture. Log aggregation and management is only one component of a security infrastructure, although has a direct dependency on the quality of the enterprise architecture. Placing security aside for a moment, the compute resources required to accomplish log aggregation, one of many actions that are required within a secure enterprise architecture, will have performance and cost implications.

Enterprise Architecture that supports Security Analytics

The collection of events that are occurring within an enterprise architecture is a great first step. There are multiple events that occur within our enterprise environment that contribute to an accurate threat analysis as well as remediation. When building an enterprise architecture, understanding all the variables that impact the outcomes, will result in a proactive security environment. Some of the variables to consider include:

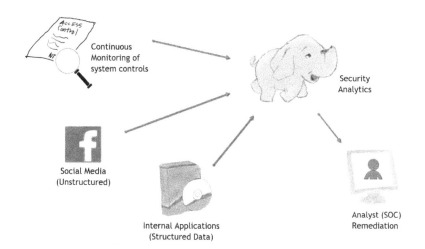

Continuous Monitoring of system controls

Security Analytics

Social Media (Unstructured)

Internal Applications (Structured Data)

Analyst (SOC) Remediation

Continuous monitoring: For many organizations continuous monitoring is a requirement of all components within the security baseline is a best practice. Continuous monitoring information helps the environment understand the health of the controls implemented within the security baseline. The continuous monitoring information is proactively consumed by the security analytics infrastructure.

Social media: Historically social media is collected as unstructured data. In a security analytics environment, external information, like social media, can be very helpful when ascertaining root cause and origin of the attack. The unstructured data from social media contributes to the security analytics environment.

Internal applications: Internal applications can be structured and unstructured data. Many internal applications are structured, meaning that they are found in columns and rows. Internal data has a direct impact on the analyst's ability to predict and remediate threats to the environment.

The security analytics engine will manage all inputs, as well as outputs to the Security Operations Center (SOC) to maintain a fluid and up-to-date security profile. A core component of an enterprise architecture is a data analytics engine for managing and providing security analytics.

Requirements for a Security Analytics Environment

A security analytics environment is similar in construction to any analytic environment. The strength of an analytics environment is the ability to set policies and rules to manage data found in the analytical database. An analytical engine with in an enterprise architecture can provide functionality that may not be realized until the solution has been installed. For example: if my environment required tenacious configuration management, an analytical infrastructure would enable me to view multiple data points and avoid challenges that may threaten the stability of my configured equipment.

Data analytics is the collection of structured and unstructured data. The data is typically targeted to provide some visualization to benefit the enterprise architecture. Many environments today deal primarily with structured data. This data may come from an application with a database, or perhaps an email server. Although unstructured data, typically found within event logs, social media, and other outlets will continue to provide critical information for the management of our business. Data analytics solutions must include a way to ingest both structured and unstructured data.

Once we sort through the lexicon, data intelligence (Big Data, Data Analytics, etc..) is the ability to leverage data to satisfy a business need. There are a lot of "big data" solutions in the market place. Some of the key technologies you want in a data analytics solution:

- Solution must support both structured and unstructured data.
- Solution should be "column based" using a column-oriented data structure, leveraging "sort" more than "index sets". This will allow you to sort through large amounts of data quickly.
- Integrated de-duplication of the data. Remember there is a lot of duplicate data, again, focus on performance.
- Solution should have close integration between structured and unstructured data allowing you to easily manage the varied data sets.
- Must have the ability to compress and encode data on the fly. Solution should allow for processing of data while in a compressed / encode state, eliminating the need to de-compress before utilizing the data set. Maximize your compute power.
- Solution must be able to operate in an "active-active" cluster, delivering zero downtime.
- Solution must provide immediate scalability and provisioning. As your data analytic needs increase, you need

to be able to simply add another x86 server and have the server automatically provisioned and added to the data analytics cluster.

- How do we visualize and organize the data?
- What is the foundation required to support big data/data analytics, and what are the changes to Infrastructure that we need to be aware of moving into the future?

Chapter 5: Functional Requirements to Get Started

Building an enterprise architecture can be riddled with challenges and wrong turns. Found herein, are some of the key components and functional requirements to get you started on your successful enterprise architecture.

Sample Enterprise Architecture - GVL

Developing an architecture without all the details related to business objectives is an impossible task. Illustrated is an example of the GVL enterprise. Perhaps you will find similarities to your environment. The GVL data center is the hub for all activity. The data center is replicated to a geo-dispersed data center. The GVL data center provides services for several organizations, to include down range

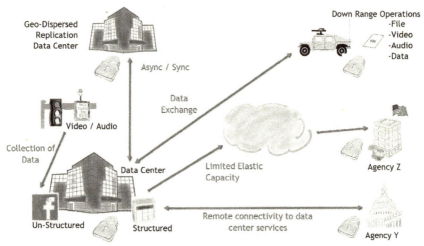

operations. Security is key concern for the environment.

All the equipment listed is built on open standards to avoid dependency upon a single vendor. Some of the technology listed within the functional requirements, will come from a specific technology vendor, like HP, although the function is generally as open as possible. There is a gentle balance between open standards and supportability. Within the GVL environment support staff are somewhat fluid, hence much of the architecture is simplified to compensate for the fluid nature of the GVL labor environment.

Building the Data Center

The following is a list of major components within the GVL data center:

1. **Storage**: One of the key attributes of the GVL storage is horizontal scalability. Horizontal scalability allows GVL to complete security control/PEN tests on a 500-node storage array, then when a new 1000 node array is required, to leverage the same security controls/PEN tests (saving cost and time). All the storage arrays used within GVL have the same operating system, providing a level of consistency found with few architectures. The GVL storage environment supports the following functional requirements, providing GVL with maximum flexibility, consistency and cost savings:
    - o Solution must support SSD, FLASH, HDD on same array controller.
    - o Solution must provide support for block, file and object environments.
    - o Solution should provide snapshots that allow for recovery of multiple restoration snapshots, not limited to the most current snapshot. Often referred to as "downstream recovery".
    - o Storage workloads must support automated workflow based on storage need and historical usage patterns.
    - o Battery backup and automated data movement for DRAM/SRAM SSD must be a default standard for all SSD technologies.
    - o Solution must provide a minimum of SSD extended warranty for 5 years.
    - o Solution must support a minimum of 3 tiers for sub-lun tiering.
    - o It is preferred that sub-lun tiering is supported by an internal card in addition to the storage processor(s).
    - o Solution must support automated tiering based on applications needs and agency defined policy.
    - o Solution tiering must support snapshot data.

- Preference will be given to solutions that provide minimal latency impact for tiering operations based on a workload provided by the organization.
- Solution must support inline deduplication.
- Inline deduplication should not require up-front space reservations.
- Preference will be given to integrated native zero reclamation hardware (not an add-on software).
- Solution must reclaim unneeded space from snapshots and remote copies.
- Deduplication must support fast lookup tables and store location pointers to accelerate data access.
- Solution must support LUN / block backup without having to travel to the server for instruction.
- Storage must allow concurrent use of adaptive flash cache and adaptive optimization sub-tiering.
- Storage must support a wide range of business requirements from transactional databases to log files on the same storage array.
- Storage solution should offer both CAPEX and OPEX acquisition models.

2. **Network infrastructure** is built upon a software defined network and secure wireless infrastructure. The environment provides numerous capabilities to the GVL environment:
   - GVL can break the hardware/vendor dependency for the network infrastructure by leveraging SDN and the elimination of some CAT5/6 networks to a secure wireless infrastructure.
   - All network infrastructure must be OpenFlow enabled allowing GVL to save money on management of the network infrastructure. OpenFlow allows for simplified integration into a SDN architecture.
   - SDN will provide the GVL enterprise architecture:
     i. Agility
        1. Rapid provisioning of network components
        2. Application focused QoS

        3. Provides a unified IP infrastructure enhancing geo-dispersed failover

  ii. Innovation

        1. Easily configure and manage a test and development environment. Isolation of network resources is greatly simplified for GVL.

  iii. Operating Expense

        1. Due to the programmable, policy driven core tenant of SDN technology, GVL will save operating expense in comparison to manual configuration of multiple network equipment throughout the enterprise.

        2. The simplicity of the SDN environment allows GVL to deploy, manage, design and scalable network like never before.

  iv. Enhanced security

        1. GVL will be able to take advantage of the consistency that SDN will bring to their environment. Consistency of deployment reduces human error, and enhances security profiles.

        2. Identified security vulnerabilities are easily remediated leveraging the centralized approach to SDN.

        3. IDS/IPS/firewall can all be integrated to enjoy the same consistency within the SDN environment.

3. Compute and delivery

    o GVL has several computer requirements:

      i. Encoding/Decoding video: GVL processes video feeds from multiple sources.

      ii. GVL has deployed multiple BladeSystem's, as well as 1U servers to handle high performance computing needs that require parallel processing expansion cards from Microns Pico.

  iii. GVL has high performance compute (HPC).

4. Systems Management
   - Systems management for GVL is built upon open standards and supports the REST API.
   - GVL performed a system management analysis that carefully aligned all the required system management tools, as well as a roadmap to migrate system management environment to support REST API.

5. Security
   - GVL has deployed a security analytics solution capable of ingesting structured and unstructured data feeds.
   - FIPS 140-2 will be used throughout the environment, coupled with Stateless Tokenization.

Down range / Remote Sites

GVL has decided to leverage converged infrastructure at all remote sites. Varied sizes are deployed dependent upon the remote site. Converged infrastructure provides the following:

1. Physical and Virtual server compatibility
2. Automated provisioning of resources based on a service catalog
3. Policy driven architecture management and provisioning
4. Integrated capacity management
5. Repeatable, Consistent, Scalable
6. OpenFlow, REST API

www.ingramcontent.com/pod-product-compliance
Lightning Source LLC
Chambersburg PA
CBHW051213050326
40689CB00008B/1293